P9-CFE-496

# Breaking into Print

## Before and After the Invention of the Printing Press

Written by

**STEPHEN KRENSKY**

Illustrated by

**BONNIE CHRISTENSEN**

Little, Brown and Company

Boston   New York   Toronto   London

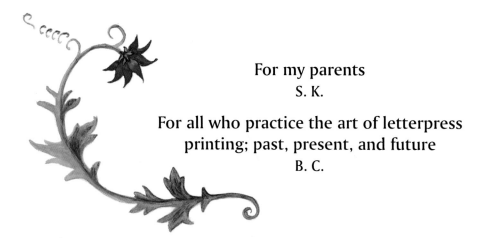

For my parents
S. K.

For all who practice the art of letterpress
printing; past, present, and future
B. C.

Text copyright © 1996 by Stephen Krensky
Illustrations copyright © 1996 by Bonnie Christensen

Special thanks to John DePol, Barbara Henry, Jim Sheridan, Ernie Dahlin, Frank Teagle Jr.,
and Peter Wells, all fine printers who have graciously shared their knowledge of the history
and techniques of letterpress printing. And thanks as well to the Pierpont Morgan Library
and the staff of the reading room.
B. C.

First Edition

Library of Congress Cataloging-in-Publication Data
Krensky, Stephen.
    Breaking into print : before and after the invention of the printing
press / written by Stephen Krensky ; illustrated by Bonnie Christensen.
— 1st ed.
        p.      cm.
    Summary: Describes the nature of books in the world before the
development of the printing press and the subsequent effect of that
invention on civilization.
    ISBN 0-316-50376-2
    1. Printing — History — Origin and antecedents — Juvenile literature.
2. Books and reading — History — Juvenile literature. 3. Gutenberg,
Johann, 1397?–1468 — Juvenile literature. 4. Printers — Germany —
Biography — Juvenile literature.   [1. Printing — History. 2. Books and
reading — History.]   I. Christensen. Bonnie, ill. II. Title.
Z126.K74   1996
686.2 — dc20                                                        95-13839


10  9  8  7  6  5  4  3  2

TOP

Published simultaneously in Canada by Little, Brown & Company (Canada) Limited

Printed in Singapore

*The illustrations in this book were created from wood engravings, in which a sharp pointed tool is used to cut an
image on the end grain of a very hard wood. (Wood cutting, in contrast, employs gouges to cut into the plank side
of the wood.) These illustrations were printed with black ink on white paper. Only the raised (uncut) areas print as
black; the cut-away areas remain white and are then painted with watercolors.*
*The illustrations are framed by painted borders in the style of illuminated manuscripts. Illuminated borders were
used both before and after the birth of printing. They often contained clues about the text, which was helpful
during early times, when most people could barely read. The borders are called illuminated because gold leaf or
paint was sometimes applied to them, illuminating, or lighting up, a book's pages.*

Of all the inventions; of all discoveries in science and art;
of all the great results in the wonderful progress of mechanical
energy and skill; the printer is the only product of civilization
necessary to the existence of free man.

Charles Dickens

In a long room with seven tables and seven windows, a French monk sat hunched over a parchment page. He dipped a goose quill in some ink and began to write. The quill made a scratching sound, like a cat clawing at a closed door.

*Parchment was made from a specially prepared animal skin, usually from sheep or goats. The best parchment, called vellum, was made from calfskin.*

*Monks worked only in natural light. The risk of fire from candles posed too great a danger to their precious manuscripts.*

*If a monastery library had 100 books, it was considered a lot. The books were so valuable, they were chained to their shelves.*

The monk worked six hours almost every day for many months. He hoped to finish before the first snow fell.

The monk was making a book.

*Charlemagne founded
many schools that taught
arithmetic, basic grammar,
and the Bible.*

*In classrooms, only teachers
had books. The students
memorized information or
took notes on wax slates.*

The monastery was a small part of a great empire, an empire with far more soldiers than books. Its emperor, Charlemagne, both read and spoke Latin, but he could write little more than his name.

Under Charlemagne's rule (800–814 A.D.) Latin was firmly established as the language of the court and education.

Charlemagne's scribes also pioneered leaving spaces between words and starting phrases with capital letters.

His scribes, however, created a new script that made writing easier to understand.

In the Middle Ages, people believed in superstitions and magic to explain things such as thunderstorms and diseases.

Rome had a population of about 500,000 in 300 A.D. After the fall of its empire, no European city had more than 20,000 people for hundreds of years.

Across the countryside, reading and writing counted for little. Few roads were free of robbers or wolves. In the villages, warring peasants lived and died without ever seeing a book.

*In England, William the Conquerer ordered a record made of the land and its owners so he could tax them accurately. This* Domesday Book *was finished in 1086.*

In time, the villages knew longer periods of peace. The peasants began to eat better and made goods to trade on market day. Successful merchants learned to read and write so that they could keep records of their business. Sometimes their children were taught as well.

Book-making shops were
centered in Paris. There,
one person wrote the text,
another added fancy letters
in red ink, and a third
painted colored borders
and decorations. Two
others checked the text for
mistakes, and another team
bound the pages together.

Books were still very
expensive. One fine book
was traded for 200 sheep,
5 measures of wheat, and
5 measures of barley.

More books were now needed, more than the
monks could manage alone. In the new book-making
guilds, many hands worked together.

Paper was invented in 105 A.D., when Ts'ai Lun reported its development to the Chinese emperor. It was made from the pulp of mulberry, bamboo, and other fibers. The paper in Europe was made from rags. It was introduced in Spain around 1150.

Block printing was first developed in Asia in the eighth century. No press was used for the printing process. After the blocks were etched and inked, paper was rubbed on them to make a print.

Many such books were made with a new material called paper. It was much cheaper than parchment and especially useful for wood or metal block printing.

*The world's oldest known printed book, a Buddhist scripture called* The Diamond Sutra, *was printed from wooden blocks in 868.*

*Korean experiments with movable type began in the 1200s.*

*The writing of Dante's* Divine Comedy *in Italian (1321) and Chaucer's* The Canterbury Tales *in English (1387) marked the rise of national languages over Latin.*

In faraway China, printers had been using paper for centuries. And around 1050, the Chinese printer Pi Sheng had invented movable type using baked clay tablets. Yet few Chinese printers were excited about the invention. Their alphabet has thousands of characters. Only in a dream could printers create so much type. And even if they managed this feat, organizing the type would turn the dream into a nightmare.

The Koreans made further progress. They were actually printing books with movable type around 1400. But their written language is as complicated as Chinese, which discouraged them from making too much of the process.

*Eyeglasses were invented around 1290 and were common by 1400. This invention enabled many more people to read by the time Gutenberg was born.*

*It was very expensive for Gutenberg to conduct his experiments. He was always borrowing money for supplies and to give himself more time to work.*

In the German town of Mainz, one young man knew nothing of Chinese or Korean printing methods. But he was interested in the idea and process of printing. His name was Johannes Gensfleisch, but he followed the old custom of taking his mother's name: Gutenberg.

As a young goldsmith and gem cutter, Gutenberg had learned how to cut steel punches and cast metal in molds. He knew which metals were hard and which were soft, which melted easily and which could take great heat without melting. Over the next few years, Gutenberg tinkered with the printing process.

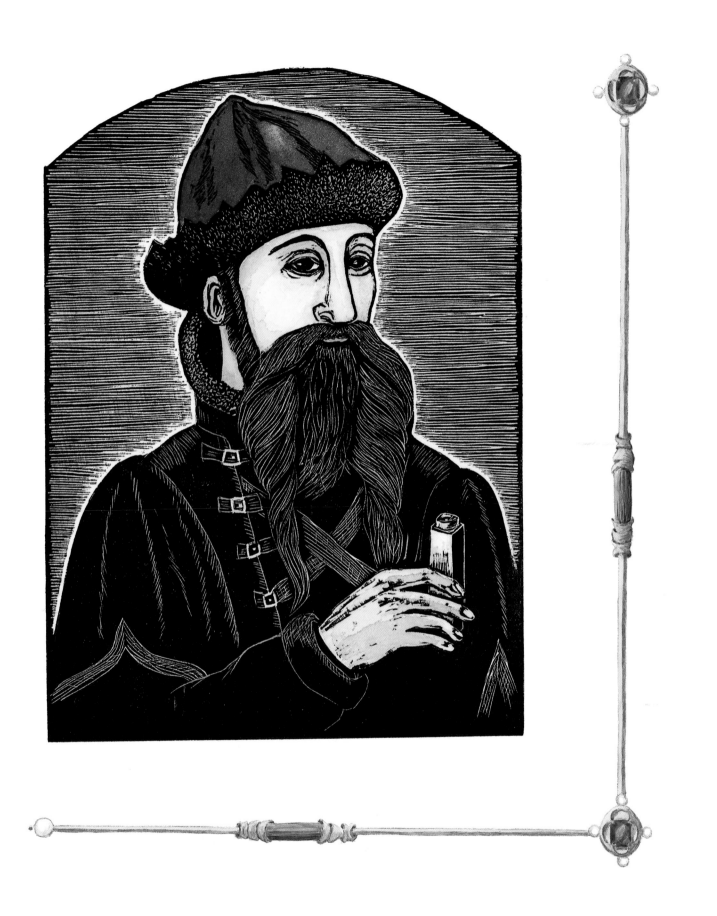

*After much experimenting, Gutenberg cast his metal type from an alloy made of 80% lead, 15% antimony, and 5% tin.*

*Gutenberg cast 290 different letters, numbers, punctuation marks, and other symbols in preparation to printing his first book.*

Although he had a simpler alphabet than the Chinese or Koreans, he still faced many obstacles. There was no room for sloppy or careless design. Printed letters had to fit as closely together as handwritten ones. Printed words had to fall in a straight line. Printed lines had to leave even spaces above and below.

Gutenberg also had to find the proper metal to cast letters and the right ink to use. If the metal was too hard, it would break too easily. If the metal was too soft, it would lose its shape too quickly. As for the ink, it could not be too thick or too thin or likely to fade over time.

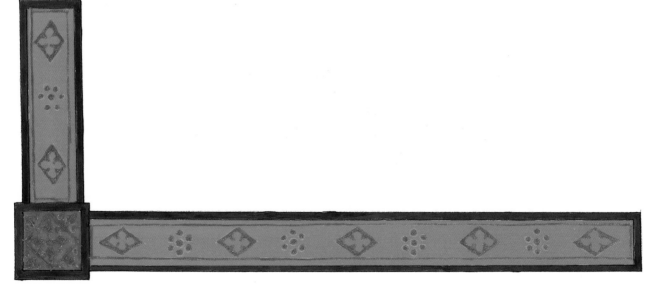

*Gutenberg's ink was made from boiled linseed oil colored with a kind of soot called lampblack.*

*Gutenberg's platen, a metal plate that flattened the paper onto the metal type, was raised and lowered by a large screw and lever.*

*Screw-style presses were used to press olives and grapes and for printing designs on cloth. They were also used for squeezing water out of damp sheets of paper.*

Gutenberg was very practical. He did not believe in reinventing things that already worked fine. So he adapted a winepress for printing. He made it taller, so that the work could be done at waist height, and he created a rolling tray for sliding the paper in and out.

Gutenberg spent almost twenty years building and tinkering. He invented adjustable molds to make letters in different widths. He found the right alloy for casting his letters. He built the upper and lower type cases for storing capital and small letters. He even created the long, grooved composing stick for quickly assembling lines of print.

*Gutenberg began working on the Bible project in 1452. It took more than three years to complete.*

*The Gutenberg Bible, published in 1456, was printed in a run of 200 copies. Though it was started with two presses, six presses were eventually used together. As many as 50 copies were printed on vellum, requiring up to 5,000 animal skins.*

Gutenberg's great project was a two-column Bible.

*[Two columns of Latin text in blackletter/Gothic typeface, reproduced from the Gutenberg Bible — Song of Songs (Canticum Canticorum)]*

Shortly before Gutenberg's Bible was completed, he lost his business when he was unable to repay a loan. Although he eventually published again, he was never free of debt. He died penniless in 1468.

It reflected everything he knew of the art of printing.

*Lower costs played a great part in the success of printing. By 1463, ten printed Bibles sold for the price of one manuscript copy.*

*In 1462, when Mainz became the site of political battles, the printers packed up their presses and spread out across Europe.*

*Englishman William Caxton was unusual among printers because his main interest was actually creating and translating books, not just running a successful business. In 1475, he produced the first printed book in English, Recuyell of the Historyes of Troye.*

*By the year 1500, there were more than 1,000 printers in Europe, and they had printed millions of books.*

Soon, other printers were building on Gutenberg's work. They added more than one ink to a page. They added illustrations to the text.

They began printing more than religious works and public notices. They began printing philosophy and poetry and stories of the imagination.

In almost no time at all, printing grew beyond the reach of one man or firm. New printers were setting up shop as fast as they could learn the craft. A generation earlier, printers had produced a single book in a few months. Now they were printing thousands of books a year.

*Despite the success of printed books, some wealthy people looked down on them as plain and coarse.*

*Although many schools were for rich students, some poor students were educated for free.*

New schools sprang up to teach people how to read. And since books were no longer rare or costly, students as well as teachers could own them. This freed the students from memorizing so much and gave them more time to think.

*When Columbus planned his trip to Asia, he studied many printed books and maps.*

*In 1543, when Copernicus first showed the solar system with the sun in the middle, a lot of people didn't believe him. They thought the earth was the center of everything.*

*When da Vinci wasn't painting, he drew up plans for inventions, including a flying machine that resembled a helicopter.*

There were geography books for Christopher Columbus and science books for Nicolaus Copernicus. And there were art and science and engineering and many other books for Leonardo da Vinci, who studied almost everything.

Reading and writing were no longer just for studious monks or highborn lords and ladies. Books were no longer chained up in private libraries or boldly sold for a king's ransom.

The printing press took learning and knowledge from just a privileged few and shared them with everyone else. And that change, more than any other act, set the stage for the modern world to come.

# The History

| | |
|---|---|
| 3500–2500 B.C. | Pictographic writing, in which simple pictures represent objects and actions, develops in the Middle East. |
| circa 3100 B.C. | Egyptians begin hieroglyphic writing, which they continue to use for more than 3,000 years. |
| circa 2360 B.C. | Babylonians create cuneiform symbols, which they write on clay tablets. |
| circa 2000 B.C. | Sheets of papyrus are developed from the Egyptian papyrus plant. Writing is done with a brushlike reed. The sheets are then rolled into scrolls. |
| 300 B.C. | Mesoamericans create scrolls on bark paper. |
| 200s B.C. | Parchment, a writing surface made from animal skin, comes into use. The split pen is developed as a writing instrument. |
| 105 A.D. | Paper is invented in China by Ts'ai Lun. |
| 200s | Romans replace the long scroll format with the codex, in which the scrolls have been cut into pages, creating the first books. |
| circa 400 | The Chinese start writing with ink. |
| 700s | The Chinese start printing with woodblocks. |
| 800s | Carolingian scribes begin leaving spaces between words to make reading easier. |
| 868 | The earliest certain date of the printing of an entire book, *The Diamond Sutra,* in China by Wang Chich. |
| 1150 | The invention of paper first reaches Europe, in Spain. |
| 1200s | The Koreans begin experimenting with movable type. |
| 1300s | Book-making guilds thrive. |
| 1390 | The first European paper mill is established in what will later become Germany. |

# of Printing

| | |
|---|---|
| Johannes Gensfleisch, or Gutenberg, is born at Mainz. | circa 1398 |
| Gutenberg's 42-line Bible is finished. | 1456 |
| The first printed book in English, *Recuyell of the Historyes of Troye,* is produced by William Caxton with Colard Mansion. | 1475 |
| More than 1,000 printers are active in Europe. | 1500 |
| The Italian printer Aldus Manutius creates a standard for mixing typefaces and for including illustrations on the printed page. | early 1500s |
| The first book is printed in the Americas, in Mexico City. | 1539 |
| The first Bible is printed in the American colonies by Samuel Green. | 1663 |
| English typefounders William Caslon and John Baskerville develop new standard type fonts. | 1700s |
| A machine for casting fonts is introduced in England. | 1822 |
| The monotype machine is patented. It combines a typewriter-like keyboard with a type casting unit to create individual letters at the stroke of a finger. | 1868 |
| The Linotype machine begins setting complete lines of "hot" type automatically in single pieces of cast lead. | 1886 |
| More efficient printing presses are developed, including self-inking capabilities and some motorization. | late 1800s |
| Phototypesetting is introduced. "Cold" type replaces "hot" type in many situations as columns of type are reproduced on photosensitive paper instead of being cast in lead. | 1950s |
| Computerized typesetting is created at video screens, storing text and illustrations on a computer disk. | 1980s |